Embracing
Difference

The Church of Ireland
in a
Plural Society

Patrick Comerford

CHURCH OF IRELAND PUBLISHING

Published by
Church of Ireland Publishing
Church of Ireland House
Church Avenue
Rathmines, Dublin 6

Designed by Susan Hood

ISBN 978-1-904884-13-2

Printed by Paceprint Trading Ltd,
Dublin, Ireland

Table of Contents

Social Justice and Theology (Republic of Ireland) Group

of the

Church of Ireland Church in Society Committee

The Church in Society Committee of the General Synod of the Church of Ireland seeks to identify, contribute to, challenge and develop areas of living today where the mission of the Church can be active and the love of God shared. It does so by seeking an informed understanding of the societies in which we live and by presenting this to the Church.

It also seeks to apply the radical expectations of the Kingdom of God to those same societies which constitute today's Ireland set in a European and global context. It aims as much to listen as to speak, to be informative and practical in the fruit of its work. It aspires to promote understanding, debate and active response to the needs of the world by members of the Church of Ireland in the name of Jesus Christ as it has been authorised by the General Synod.

The sub-groups of the Church in Society Committee are authorised to issue statements and reports in their own names. The mission of the Social Justice and Theology Group (Republic of Ireland) is: 'To provide where possible pro-active, as well as reflective theological comment, on contemporary issues of social justice within the Republic of Ireland, and where relevant to make suggestions on possible courses of action'.

The Group works by having a small core of three members, the chairperson (Very Revd Gordon Wynne, Dean of Leighlin), his deputy (Mr Lachlan Cameron) and a secretary (Ms Fiona Forrest-Bills) co-opting fully those whose expertise bears upon the subject under study. In this case, the entire authorship belongs to Canon Patrick Comerford, and the Group is delighted to facilitate the work that he has produced.

Forward

by

Lachlan Cameron

I N THE NINETEENTH AND TWENTIETH CENTURIES, Ireland has been associated more with emigration than immigration, but, as Canon Patrick Comerford points out, there was also a steady stream of immigrants over this period. As these immigrants were largely similar in ethnic and cultural background to the existing population, the psychological impact was limited. With the growth of prosperity in Ireland, the extension of the European Union, and improved methods of transportation, a much wider range of immigrants has appeared and public concern has grown.

These concerns of the public are genuine and strongly felt, not only in Ireland but in other countries receiving such immigrants. It is not enough to dismiss their fears as ignorance or racism; they must be faced and openly discussed. If they are only repressed, they will grow and become more embittered.

The task of The Church in Society Committee is to identify issues, provide information and equip the Church to look at these problems from a Christian point of view and Patrick's document provides us with a good basis for such discussion.

While the views expressed are his own and would not necessarily always represent those of the committee, he provides a knowledgeable and detailed scriptural analysis of the issues and has produced a good range of topics for use by church groups. There is, in addition, a valuable list of resources and contact organisations. We feel that this document deserves a wider audience and are happy to put it forward as a contribution towards a solution of the problems.

Lachlan Cameron is a member of the Social Justice and Theology Panel (Republic of Ireland) of the Church in Society Committee, and a retired educationalist.

Note on biblical references:

All of the Scripture passages in this study guide are from the *New Standard Revised Version Bible* © 1993 and 1998 by the Division of Christian Education of the National Council of Churches of America.

Introduction

'You shall also love the stranger'
(Deuteronomy 10:19)

THE FACE OF IRELAND IS CHANGING, and is changing dramatically. Today, the second most common language of the Republic is no longer Irish – it is Polish. Poles make up the largest single ethnic majority in the state, and the latest census figures show at least 63,000 Polish nationals living in the Irish state today. In recent years the Poles, Lithuanians and Latvians have pushed the Chinese into fourth place, but Chinese remains one of the largest minority language groups, especially in the greater Dublin area, where there may be a Chinese population of up to 60,000 people.

Recent research at the National University of Ireland Maynooth shows that more than 167 different languages – from Acholi to Zulu – are used by 160 nationalities among the people in Ireland as their everyday first language of choice. Ireland has become a multilingual society, so that the 2006 census was conducted in 13 languages. Apart from English and Irish, these languages were: Arabic, Chinese, Czech, French, Latvian, Lithuanian, Polish, Portuguese, Romanian, Russian and Spanish. In addition, information was also available in Estonian, Magyar (Hungarian), Slovak, Turkish and Yoruba.

If Ireland has become a multilingual and multicultural society, then it has also become a multi-faith society. Although Muslims in Ireland do not form one single ethnic minority, Islam has already become the third largest faith grouping in our society, with the number of Muslims equal to – if not greater than – the combined figures for our Methodist and Presbyterian neighbours.

The share of foreign-born people living in the Republic of Ireland is about 11%, although this figure includes 1.3% born in Northern Ireland. The Central Statistic Office estimates that 9% of immigrants are now Chinese, and 8% are nationals from Central and Eastern European countries.

The European Commission said recently that immigrants have been good for the Irish economy, contributing to the country's excellent economic performance. The number of foreign workers far outweighs the number of refugees or asylum seekers, with an estimated 180,000 foreign workers employed in jobs that boost our industry and have helped make Ireland one of the richest economies in Europe. These figures are a striking testimony to the recent success of the Irish economy and reflect the increasing availability of relatively well-paid work.

All the predictions are that this trend will continue, with the

Republic needing significant numbers of immigrants in the future.

However, migrants in Ireland appear to suffer disproportionately more from social problems and discrimination, including homelessness, than the rest of Irish society. A recent newspaper survey showed that foreigners in Ireland are more likely than the rest of us to be murdered, to end up in jail, to be killed on the roads, to be injured at home or in work, or to find themselves homeless.

The survey shows:

- Of the 58 murders in Ireland in 2005, 10 of the victims were foreigners, including four Lithuanians. In the previous year, when there were 44 murders, six of the victims were foreigners, including three Lithuanians.
- One in five of the 1,804 people jailed in the Republic in 2004 were non-nationals. More than one-in-four prisoners are thought to be foreigners.
- Non-nationals are more likely to be the victims of crime than Irish-born people, according to the Central Statistics Office.
- Racism is a common experience for many of our immigrants.
- Of the 33 people killed on the roads in the first month of 2006, almost a quarter of them were non-nationals, mainly Poles.

- The Health and Safety Authority has pointed to the worrying trend indicated by foreign workers being the victims of more than one-in-seven fatal accidents in the workplace.
- A disproportionate number of children admitted to our hospitals are the children of asylum seekers.

A report commissioned by the Health Service Executive recently highlighted flaws in the services in Ireland for separated children seeking asylum. More than 2,000 such children have been reunited with adults in Ireland since 1999. However, 250 other separated children have gone missing from State care in a four-year period.

The response to new immigrants, migrant workers, asylum seekers and refugees can be very warm and welcoming in many places. But these statistics show that the new strangers in our midst suffer a disproportionate number of problems in the workplace, and from attitudes on the streets. They suffer as children in the home, or as families seeking housing, and those difficulties often lead to other problems too – problems that are reflected in the figures for road deaths and prisoners.

According to the Irish Refugee Council, the climate in Ireland is very hostile for many immigrants including asylum-seekers. Of course there is a duty for politicians, employers, the public services and the trade unions, to face these problems. But has the Church a role in welcoming the stranger in our midst? What part can we play in making those people who want to live among us feel welcome, feel at home?

This guide first of all asks who are the strangers in our midst? Who are these new neighbours that we need to get to know? We then look at some of the myths that fuel racism and xenophobia. We look at what the Bible has to say about welcoming the stranger, and there are some Bible studies that can be used in diocesan or parish groups or in schools and community groups to begin discussing our own responsibilities in this sphere. This is followed by some resources for prayer or suitable for liturgical use. Then there are some practical hints and ideas about how to get to know our new neighbours. Finally, there is a section providing resources, listing organisations and publications that can help you continue this important ministry in the life of the Church.

Acknowledgments

The author wishes to gratefully acknowledge the support of the Social Justice and Theology Group and all in Church of Ireland Publishing who assisted in bringing this publication to fruition. The administrative support of Fiona Forrest-Bills, editorial work on earlier drafts by Lucy Connolly, and the editorial oversight and design work of Dr Susan Hood is greatly appreciated.

1

The stranger in our midst

Shattering some myths

TWO COMMON MISPERCEPTIONS ARE PROMINENT in any discussion about the strangers we are called to welcome in our midst in Ireland today. One is the notion that immigration and migration are new phenomena in Irish society. Others think that asylum seekers and refugees make up the largest number of foreign nations and immigrants in the Republic of Ireland today, although the statistics show that this is simply not so. And there are fears among many about job security, wages, standards in the workplace and social protection; those fears are closely linked to some of the worst scaremongering about immigration, yet they do not stand up to scrutiny.

Great changes in any society, including social and economic changes, bring uncertainties and fears which can find expression in irrational and unfounded emotions. In Ireland today, we are experiencing unprecedented and very visible changes in our society. The number of new immigrants is visible in the workplace, on the streets, in shops and in our towns and suburbs. At the same time, many companies are relocating to countries in Asia and Eastern Europe, where labour costs are lower. None of these changes is unique to Ireland – they are all part of the globalisation that is affecting every society and every economy around the world.

But when people allow their fears to be transformed into prejudice and hatred, how many of us are aware of the causes of these changes in Irish life? How many of us know how to integrate our perceptions of these changes into our understanding of Irish life built on the experience of past generations? And how often are we able to count the positive benefits these changes are bringing to our families and our localities?

Migration in Irish history

Of course, migration has been a common experience of Irish society, even before the Great Famine in the 1840s. The Church of Ireland was enriched in the 17th and 18th century with the arrival of Huguenot refugees from Paris and Palatine and Hessian settlers from Germany who were quickly integrated into the life and fabric of the Church.

Before the Great Famine, Irish Protestants were the largest group of emigrants to North America, and the contribution of those early Irish emigrants contributed immensely to the shape and spirituality of the Anglican Church in

Canada and the Episcopal Church in the United States.

Emigration was so strong in the 1950s that the population of the Republic fell to its lowest ever level in 1961. Not enough people were living in the Republic to cope with the economic expansion of the 1970s and the need for more workers, and that decade was marked by a net inward migration. Emigration once again became a feature of Irish life in the 1980s, but since 1991, Ireland has seen more people coming to live in this society than are leaving it. Without immigration and the inflow of foreign workers, it would not have been possible to maintain the momentum of economic growth introduced by the Celtic Tiger.

Initially, this inward migration consisted mainly of returning Irish emigrants, forced to leave the island in the lean years of the 1980s. But in more recent years there has been a steady inflow of non-Irish people seeking to meet the shortage of labour that became obvious with virtually full employment in the late 1990s.

The age profile of the Irish population is likely to rise significantly over the next 30 years, so that by 2036, the over 65s among us could account for almost 22% of the total population. This implies a significant increase in the dependency ratio, and figures like this have serious implications for pension requirements and for fiscal policies. To

15

fund this ageing population the tax burden will have to increase significantly, unless we develop a policy of welcoming more immigrants and foreign workers.

According to the economist Moore McDowell, writing in the *Irish Independent,* 'unless we sharply reverse the birth rate, our current standard of living depends on attracting immigrants, especially those with a high endowment of human capital – those we call asylum seekers'. How we welcome those immigrants, foreign workers and asylum seekers, how we make them feel at home, and how we encourage them to stay for long enough a period in Ireland will have beneficial or detrimental effects on the Irish economy. Even a selfish disposition would say we need to welcome the stranger, if only to keep taxes down and to ensure the government has enough funds to pay all our pensions.

Who is my neighbour?

It is sad to hear people at times saying that Europe or Ireland is being flooded by refugees. The reverse is the case. The overwhelming majority of the world's refugees are in the least developed countries. In 2005, the United Nations High Commissioner for Refugees estimated that there were over 9.2 million refugees in the world. Sub-Saharan Africa hosts almost one-third of those people, over 2.7 million; North Africa, the Middle East and Central

Asia hosts another one-third, more than 2.7 million people. On the other hand, Europe hosts only a quarter of the world's refugees, or 2.3 million people. Taken together, Pakistan, Afghanistan and Iran host more refugees than all of Europe. And the single biggest category of refugees in Europe is the almost 600,000 people in Former Yugoslavia who are classified as 'internally displaced persons'.

The myth that the world is being flooded by refugees is sometimes propped up by claims that the majority of our refugees or asylum seekers are Africans. But the largest number of refugees in the world – over 2 million people – comes from Afghanistan. In Ireland, the top five countries of origin for new asylum seekers at the beginning of 2006 were: Nigeria (784), Somalia (199), Romania (187), Afghanistan (90), and Sudan (74). In the previous year, the five leading countries of origin of new asylum applicants were: Nigeria (1,418), Somalia (1,038), Romania (286), Sudan (264) and Afghanistan (141).

As these figures show, the numbers of people newly seeking asylum in Ireland – as in many other western countries – is dropping steadily. At the same time, the number of migrant workers coming to Ireland is growing swiftly. It is important to distinguish between the different categories of strangers and foreigners who are now in our midst. The Immigrant Council of Ireland places them in the following groupings:

- Migrant workers
- Self-employed or business people
- International students
- Non-economically active persons
- Parents and siblings of Irish citizens' children
- Persons granted leave to remain
- Family members of migrants and Irish nationals
- Persons residing in the state without permission
- Visitors

In any one year, the largest category of strangers to arrive in the state is tourists – about six million people visited this country in 2004 as tourists. But they are not regarded as immigrants because most of them do not intend to stay here. Nevertheless, they are strangers, and we must welcome them.

Who are our new neighbours?

Figures from the Central Statistics Office indicate the number of foreign-born nationals living in the Republic of Ireland is about 457,000 out of a total population of 4.1 million. More than one-third of 70,000 immigrants to Ireland in the 12-month period up to April 2005 came from the new accession states in the European

Union: 17% (11,900) of those immigrants came from Poland and 9% (6,300) from Lithuania. These numbers are totally outweighed by the 19,000 returning Irish citizens (27%), and close to the number of UK nationals moving here (6,900 or 10%). Of the 50,100 people who came to Ireland as immigrants in 2004, one-third (16,900) had Irish nationality – they were returning Irish emigrants, their children, or people from Northern Ireland.

Two-thirds of all the non-Irish nationals living in the Republic of Ireland come from the 15 member states that European Union before the latest expansion, or from the other member states of the European Economic Area, including Iceland, Norway, Liechtenstein and Switzerland. Those people enjoy an unrestricted right to migrate within the EEA states and the right to take up employment in Ireland. And among the other one-third of non-Irish nationals living in the Republic most are workers who have come here seeking employment even though they do not have an automatic right to work in Ireland. Newly-arrived migrant workers now make up a far larger community in Ireland than the total number of people who sought refuge here in the last decade.

Migrant workers and the economy

Migrant workers are found in all sectors of the economy,

but a large number of these workers are concentrated in unskilled or low-skill employment in services, catering, agriculture and fisheries, and industry. The largest single category of migrant workers is from Poland, closely followed by Latvia, Lithuania, the Philippines, Romania, South Africa, Ukraine, Australia, China, the Czech Republic and Malaysia. In other words, the majority of migrant workers from outside the original 15 EU member states and the EEA come from Central and Eastern Europe, and the vast majority of those come from countries that are EU member states.

The opening of the Irish labour market in May 2004 to citizens of the new EU member states was a major change. Because data on the impact of immigration on the labour market are not being gathered currently, it is difficult to know exactly what is going on. This gives room for scaremongering and unfounded prejudice. There is no statistical evidence that immigration is driving wages down. But, undoubtedly, this change has increased the opportunities for unscrupulous employers to exploit a vulnerable sector of the workforce. But the answer cannot lie with blaming the victim. One solution lies in a more rigorous enforcement of existing laws on wages and conditions and, perhaps, even more onerous penalties for those who flout them. Immigration need not erode standards: parishes can encourage trade unions to recruit new immigrants in the workplace so their rights are protected and to ensure they receive fair wages. We must all watch out for those who are vulnerable and in danger of exploitation.

Irish economists forecast continued growth in the economy but they say that 300,000 more immigrant workers will be needed over the next decade if Ireland's potential is to be realized. We can compare this with neighbouring Britain, which has been absorbing even larger numbers of EU migrants – about 16,000 a month – and their productivity has contributed $800 million to the British economy, according to government figures.

When he was Minister for Social Affairs, Seamus Brennan, pointed out that Ireland will need 50,000 workers from outside the state each year for the next 12 years if current levels of economic growth are to be maintained. Quoting statistics from the Central Statistics Office, Minister Brennan said it was important that workers from abroad were made to feel welcome in Ireland, just as the Irish had been when they helped to build other countries.

The European Commission said recently that immigrants have been good for the Irish economy, contributing to the country's excellent economic performance. The number of foreign workers far outweighs the number of refugees or asylum seekers, with an estimated 180,000 foreign workers employed in jobs that boost our industries. They have helped make Ireland one of the richest economies in Europe.

Many migrant workers do not want to be integrated or absorbed into Irish society. They want to feel welcome, but they hope to return home at some future date. They keep in touch with family, social and sporting life at home, and so Polish, Romanian and Russian-language newspapers are now commonplace on many newsstands in inner-city shops in Dublin. They are often homesick, and want food and news from home. They want to be welcomed, and welcomed warmly. But many hope some day to return home again.

The experience of Spain and Portugal in the past shows that migrant workers from EU member states tend to start drifting home as their home economies begin to improve. The skills, experience and capital they have acquired in the intervening years give them a competitive advantage in the workforce and in the housing market. If these trends are repeated, then we could lose many of our new workers from Bulgaria, the Czech Republic, Latvia, Lithuania, Poland and Romania. Within a few years we could be hoping for vastly greater numbers of immigrant workers ... but this time they will have to come from outside the EU. Very few of the strangers who come to Ireland are asylum seekers. There were only 4,860 asylum seekers in 2005.

Immigrants, racism and exploitation

The Racist Incident Reporting Procedure of the National Consultative Committee on Racism and Interculturalism has documented racist incidents directed at migrant workers in Ireland. The types of racist incidents ranged from verbal and physical abuse to discrimination in accessing goods or services or in their employment. The Council of Europe watchdog on racism, the European Commission on Racism and Intolerance (ECRI) *Second report on Ireland* stated that 'more attention needs to be paid to non-citizen workers as members of Irish society rather than just economic entities and that measures should be taken to reflect this approach, such as for example the introduction of a wider range of work permit types to meet different situations and wider possibilities for family reunification'.

While many migrant workers with work permits and visas enjoy adequate conditions of employment, there are also increasing reports of migrant workers experiencing poor and exploitative conditions arising from the actions or inactions of a number of rogue employers and employment agencies. By its very nature, the extent of this is difficult to assess as workers in such positions are slow to come forward, afraid of losing their employment or jeopardising the employment of their colleagues. In some cases, through language barriers or lack of access to impartial information, migrant workers may not know about employment and equality rights in Ireland. There has been an increase in the number of complaints to the Equality Tribunal taken under the race ground of the Employment Equality Act 1998. Polish, Hungarian and Serbian workers have been at the centre of complaints about exploitation and low wages in major sectors of the Irish economy.

The Migrant Rights Centre has reported a huge increase in the number of workers seeking its help because they are being mistreated. They include groups of workers as far afield as Cavan, Laois, Mayo, Meath, Monaghan and Tipperary. Workers are entitled to a minimum hourly wage of €7.80, but the Migrants Rights Centre says some migrant workers in Ireland are being paid as low as €2.50-€4.50 an hour, told to work excessive hours, and paid no compensation for overtime. In many cases they are not given wage slips, and it is a common complaint that money is deducted illegally from payments. Many of these workers remain voiceless because they live in fear of losing their jobs which are often tied to their accommodation.

Some of our new communities

Recent research at the National University of Ireland Maynooth shows that over 167 different languages are used in everyday conversation by people living in Ireland. The latest census was carried out in Irish and English and in 11 foreign languages that are now commonly heard on our streets and in our schools and shops: Arabic, Chinese, Czech, French, Latvian, Lithuanian, Polish, Portuguese, Romanian, Russian and Spanish, with additional information available in Estonian, Magyar (Hungarian), Slovak, Turkish and Yoruba.

The most visible new identities in the State include Poles, who, according to some figures, may account for up to 400,000 people living in Ireland today; people from the Baltic states, including perhaps 100,000 Lithuanians and between 25,000 and 50,000 Latvians, but a surprisingly small number of people from Estonia; the Chinese; the Nigerian and other African communities; Muslims, who do not constitute a separate ethnic grouping and many of whom are from Ireland; and the Romanians.

1. The Polish community

Poles make up the largest single ethnic majority in state, and although may be about 100,000 Poles here with PPS numbers, some trade union estimates say there may be from 200,000 to 400,000 Polish nationals living in the Irish state today. According to a controversial recent article in the Polish edition of *Newsweek*, 'Newbridge [Co Kildare] has become a capital of Polish emigration. Even though there were just 10 Poles living there four years ago, today Polish people comprise half of this town's 30,000 strong population'.

About 1,000 Poles attend the Polish-language Mass each Sunday in Saint Michan's Church in Dublin city centre, and as many as 60 Poles show up each day at Capuchin Day Centre there. The Polish community in Ireland has its own Polish-language newspaper in Ireland, *StrefaEire* (Irish Zone), which began publishing in November 2005, with Tomasz Wybranowski as its editor, while Dublin's *Evening Herald* produces a weekly supplement in Polish, and a local newspaper in Limerick carries a weekly column in Polish. A Polish weekend school, which opened in Dublin in October 2005 with 80 pupils, helps the children of Polish families who are here temporarily keep pace with language and history requirements back home. Since the summer of 2005, Bus Eireann has been running a daily bus service from Busarus in Dublin to the Polish capital, Warsaw. There are Polish shops, cafes and bars in many cities and towns throughout the island.

2. Our Baltic neighbours

Anecdotal evidence suggests that the second largest ethnic group in the Republic now comes from Latvia. Since Latvia joined the EU in May 2004, up to 100,000 people have emigrated from Latvia, a country of 2.3 million. Many of those are in the United Kingdom or Sweden, but at least 25,000 to 30,000 are in Ireland, and some unofficial figures put the Latvian community in Ireland anywhere between 25,000 and 50,000.

The Irish mushroom industry, which is worth more than €130 million a year, employs 3,000 mainly Latvian and Lithuanian workers, many of them said to be the victims of gross exploitation. Latvia is a traditionally Lutheran country, and unofficial statistics indicate up to 50% of the population belongs to the Lutheran Church of Latvia. The Lutheran Church has observer status in the Porvoo Communion, but is not a full member. Nevertheless, the close links between the Church of Ireland the Lutheran churches in the Baltic states must leave us with a special pastoral responsibility for Latvian Lutherans in Ireland. Latvia's Ambassador to Ireland, Indulis Ābelis, and the Latvian embassy in Dublin work with immigrant workers to preserve their Latvian spirit and culture, and the Latvian school in Dublin serves a growing Latvian migrant population.

In December 2005, 70,000 protesters marched in Dublin to protest against the plan by Irish Ferries to replace its crews with Latvians workers employed for half the minimum wage. The company was reflagging its ships to circumvent Irish wage laws, but the trade union leaders who organised the protest were firm in rejecting suggestions that the organisers were hostile to immigrants. But after the rally, one American newspaper carried the headline: 'For Irish, Latvians fill role of bogeymen'.

Back in Latvia, Latvians fear that the current exodus is destroying the country's social fabric. The problem of migrant workers leaving for Ireland is so topical that the Latvian commercial TV channel, LNT, developed a recent series of reports about the Irish Latvian experience. Media reports in Latvia and in Ireland and Britain recently highlighted the story of one Latvian immigrant, Jekabs Nakums. Back home, he is a well-known sports figure, having come fifth in the biathlon at the Winter Olympics eight years ago. Last year, he announced that, just like many other Latvians, he was heading to Ireland to find work. His current job is as a car cleaner, based in Naas, and travelling around the Dublin area. He is also training to be a fitness instructor.

In the Latgale farming region in eastern Latvia, nearly every third home sits empty because their occupants have left to pick mushrooms in Ireland. Laima Muktupavela, a mother of four who left more than three years ago, moved into a three-room house near Dublin with 11 other Latvians and picked mushrooms from 6 a.m. to sunset. She says the farm owner forbade the Latvian workers to wear gloves and the mushrooms quickly turned her fingers black. She earned about €215 a week – more than 1½ times the monthly minimum wage back home. When Muktupavela returned to Latvia, she wrote a book about her experiences, *The Mushroom Covenant,* which tapped into the national fear about the growing exodus of Latvians to Ireland, and it became a best seller. 'There is hardly a family left in this country who hasn't lost a son or daughter or mother or father to the mushroom farms of Ireland', she told a reporter.

Latvian parents who emigrate to Ireland to pick mushrooms often leave their children behind, creating a new generation of 'mushroom orphans'. The children live with their grandparents or are shuffled back and forth from Latvia to Ireland. In Riga, more than 100 children aged 14 or younger are living alone or with family friends, according to the International Organisation for Migration. There was a national outcry when a seven-year-old girl got lost on the way home from school and it was discovered that her parents were living in Ireland.

The migration has given Latvia a short-term economic lift – the World Bank estimates that funds sent home by migrants amount to $230 million annually – but economists say this benefit is being offset by a brain drain in key sectors such as construction, nursing and medicine. And while EU membership has helped spur a development boom in Riga, construction companies complain that there are too few qualified workers. Marcis Nikolajevs, managing director of an association of Latvian building contractors, said that companies were being forced to import workers from neighbouring Ukraine and Belarus. The association is considering flying in temporary building workers from Ghana. A shortage of doctors and nurses has also gripped the country because so many have left to work in hospitals in Denmark, Norway and Sweden, where the pay is better. Latvia's economics minister, Krisjanis Karins, says the only way to stem the migration is to close the wage gap with the EU's richer countries.

Irish officials say the influx of Latvians has been good for the economy since Baltic workers work hard and are willing to take low-level jobs that the upwardly mobile Irish avoid. 'The free movement of Eastern Europeans has been good for the Irish economy', Tim Mawe, Ireland's ambassador to Latvia, told the *International Herald Tribune*. But he added: 'I don't think it's a good thing when you have Latvian brain surgeons doing McDonald's jobs'. Laima Muktupavela believes her time in Ireland has helped to turn her into an independent person and literary star. She is now writing her fifth novel and is working on a film about the migration. She notes that Latvia's experience has deep parallels with that of Ireland, a once-poor farming country where migration was once common, but one that has become an economic powerhouse and magnet for immigration.

3. The Chinese community

The Chinese remains one of the largest minority language groups, especially in the greater Dublin area, where there may be a Chinese population of up to 30,000 or 40,000 people. As many as 60,000 Chinese now live in Ireland, the Chinese Premier, Wen Jiabao, said during a visit to Dublin in May 2004. In addition, there are about 10,000 Chinese residents in Northern Ireland, where they are the largest and most dispersed ethnic minority group and the community is growing at a faster rate than the general population.

The history of the Chinese ommunity traces its roots to the early 1960s, when the first Chinese arrived in large numbers, encouraged additionally by a growth in demand for Chinese restaurants and Chinese food. The number of Chinese students in Ireland has increased significantly from a few hundred in 1997 to more than 30,000 now. Under work-study visas, students can legally work up to 20 hours a week. Faced with high living costs, many work far longer hours, sometimes dropping their studies or staying to work long after their visas have expired. Garda sources say many of the students coming here have little interest in learning English and are coming to Ireland as economic migrants.

A high proportion of the Chinese residents in Northern Ireland were born outside Northern Ireland, with seven out of ten born in Hong Kong. Other places of origin include China, Malaysia and Singapore. However, no figures are available for the Chinese community in the Republic, and no study has yet been made of the patterns of Chinese migration into the state. Nevertheless, some experts believe the majority of Chinese-speaking people in the Republic are now Mandarin-speaking, while the majority 80% to 90% of Chinese-speakers in Northern Ireland speak Cantonese, the language of many of the Chinese from mainland Hong Kong, the New Territories, Malaysia and Singapore.

Although little is known about the religious beliefs and practices of many of the Chinese in Ireland, there are seven Chinese-speaking Roman Catholic priests studying in Dublin, one deacon, and five nuns. There is a monthly

Mass in Chinese at 2pm on the second Sunday of each month in Saint Paul's Church, Arran Quay, Dublin. In addition, there are two ethnic Chinese evangelical churches in Dublin. The Dublin University Far Eastern Mission, one of the oldest mission agencies in the Church of Ireland, works closely with many Chinese students and immigrants.

The celebration of the Chinese New Year is one of the most important festivals within the Chinese community in Ireland. This celebration falls between late January and mid-February, on the first day of the month of the Chinese Lunar calendar. Preparations for the festival usually begin two weeks in advance, as business accounts are settled and households are swept clean. Joining in festivals such as the Chinese New Year or enjoying Chinese food are two ways of getting to know your Chinese neighbours.

Some of the main difficulties currently confronting the Chinese community in Ireland relate to the language barrier, difficulties in obtaining equitable access to health and social services, welfare, housing provision and education, experiences of social isolation, and experiences of racial harassment and discrimination. A survey of Chinese teenagers born in Northern Ireland from South and East Belfast shows that an alarming 100% had experienced some kind of racially motivated attacks, both verbal and physical. Many admitted that they felt treated as unwelcome visitors, despite the fact they were born in Ireland.

4. Nigerians and other Africans in Ireland

Despite their high visibility, the number of Nigerians in Ireland is far lower than many of the public estimates. A report from the Irish Council of Churches estimates that of the 30,000 or so Africans in the Republic, about 20,000 are Nigerians.

Nigerians say they suffer racism not only from Irish-born people but also from other African-born residents in Ireland too. According to the director of the Irish Refugee Council, Peter O'Mahony, the single greatest obstacle to an asylum seeker obtaining leave to remain in Ireland on humanitarian grounds is Nigerian origin. Yet this small community makes an impressive and positive contribution to life in Ireland today. Rotimi Adebari elected mayor of Portlaoise in June 2007, is Ireland's first black mayor. Tokie Laotan, originally from Lagos, has a degree in international relations and stood as independent candidate in Galway City in the last local elections. Paul Osikoya, another independent candidate in Galway, works with the Galway Youth Federation. Benedicta Attoh, who was an independent candidate in Dundalk, is a business education graduate working for the Depaul Trust in Dublin. Revd Obbina Ulogwara is a Nigerian Anglican priest from Lagos now working in the Church of Ireland parishes of Whitechurch and Tallaght in Dublin. Stella Obe, also from Nigeria, was recently commissioned as a Diocesan Reader in Dublin – the first African-born reader in the diocese. Other African communities in Ireland include people from DR Congo, Sierra Leone, Somalia and Sudan.

5. Muslims in Ireland

Although Muslims in Ireland do not form one single ethnic minority, Islam has already become the third largest faith grouping in our society, with the number of Muslims equal to – if not greater than – the combined figures for our Methodist and Presbyterian neighbours. Today, there are between 20,000 and 30,000 Muslims living in the Republic of Ireland. Many of the Muslims in Ireland are European-born – from Britain, France, Turkey, Bosnia, Kosovo, Albania, and a large proportion of Muslims in Ireland are Irish-born. Some Muslims in Ireland come from Arab countries, including Egypt, Libya, Algeria, Palestine, Iraq and Morocco. But many are not Arabs, and the other countries of origin among members of the Muslim community include Pakistan, India, Iran, Malaysia, China, and Indonesia, which is largest Muslim country in the world.

The depth and scope of anti-Islamic feeling since the 9/11 attacks in the United States on 11 September 2001 is so strong in many places that it is akin to racism and is now known generally as 'Islamophobia'. Many of our Muslim neighbours wonder how they can be victims of such hatred from people who call themselves Christian, and they point to the many similarities between Christianity and Islam, including belief in the one God, belief in his prophets, among whom they count Jesus Christ, and belief in God's revelation through Scripture, including the Torah (the first five books of the Bible), the Psalms and the Gospels.

The incident in Saint Patrick's Cathedral, Dublin, in May 2006, when a group of refugees and asylum seekers from Afghanistan sought to draw attention to their stories, posed many dilemmas for the Church and for the Gardai. But it also illustrated how many Muslims believe the Church and Christians ought to be symbols of hope for the stranger who believes he or she is being oppressed.

Now that there are many Muslim children in our parish schools, Muslims on the staff of our hospitals, and Muslims living on our streets, we need to get to know them and to let them know they are welcome. In return, we may be challenged about our Christian faith, but a challenge should be seen not as a threat but as a gift, offering to deepen and strengthen the foundations of our own faith and beliefs.

6. Romanians in Ireland

There may be more than 20,000 Romanians living in Ireland today. They often complain that they are all categorised as Gypsies or Roma people, but while many of the 2,000 or so members of the Roma community in Ireland come from other countries in Central and Eastern Europe, a report from the Irish Council of Churches shows that there is little or no interaction between the Romanian and Roma communities.

The Romanian population is largely Dublin-based, and there are Romanian restaurants in Dublin in Bolton Street and Lucan. The Romanian Orthodox Parish of the Exaltation of the Holy Cross now uses the former Church of Ireland parish church, Christ Church, Leeson Park, there are Romanian-language masses for the Roman Catholic minority within this community in two Dublin churches in Sean McDermott Street and Rathmines, and there is a large number of smaller Romanian Pentecostalist, Baptist and Adventist churches in Dublin and other parts of Ireland.

New churches in Ireland

Many of the new communities in Ireland have brought with them their own religious identity. The new churches within the Orthodox tradition include the Greek, Romanian and Russian Orthodox Churches, the Coptic Orthodox Church and the Indian Orthodox Church. These communities embrace many people from beyond the narrow ethnic boundaries that might be indicated by their names. The Greek Orthodox Church includes Greeks, Cypriots, Arabs, and many people from Eastern Europe, North Africa and the Middle East. The Romanian Orthodox Church also includes people from Moldova, Ukraine and other parts of Eastern Europe. The Russian Orthodox Church includes Russians as well as Belarussians, Ukrainians and people from the Baltic states within the EU. The Coptic Church includes Egyptians, Ethiopians and Sudanese. The Romanian community includes a number of small Pentecostalist, Adventist and independent Baptist churches and a Greek Catholic parish in communion with Rome.

The African immigrants have brought their expressions of Christianity with them too, and over the course of years some Irish people have also joined these churches. These churches often help their people to maintain their ethnic identity and their connections with home. They include the

French-speaking Kimbanguist Church, which originated in the Congo.

Many of the African churches have high Sunday attendances, and some of them – including the Redeemed Church of God, the Christ Apostolic Church and the Mountain of Fire Ministries – have a number of branches throughout the island. The Redeemed Church of God is the largest of all the black ethnic minority churches in Ireland. The parent church is in Nigeria, and there are at least 17 branches in the Republic, with Sunday church attendances in their hundreds. Other Nigerian-led churches include the Christ Apostolic Church, Mountain of Fire Ministries, Christ Apostolic Church International, the Cherubim and Seraphim Church.

These churches need our friendship and may even need to draw on our experience. When members of these churches find themselves in hospital or in prison, can their pastors turn to our clergy for advice about chaplaincy services? When their children want to go to school, which school should they go to? When their young adults want to train as teachers, where will they go? The experience of the Church of Ireland is not a legacy to keep in cold storage and archives, but a gift that can be shared with others and help to reach their full potential as Christians and as citizens.

The need for more immigrants

Despite the mixed feelings of some people, a new study says Ireland will need skilled immigrants to fill some 400,000 jobs in the next five years. In the long run, however, we must also welcome the stranger because God tells us to welcome the stranger in our midst.

By welcoming the stranger we can also learn more about ourselves, and discover more about the cultural riches we are being offered as gifts. But we can also grow in faith and discipleship.

2

What the Bible says about welcoming the stranger

THE ANCIENT ISRAELITES ARE COMMANDED to love God and to love their neighbours, but they are also commanded to love the stranger. They are reminded constantly that their ancestors had been strangers and aliens, and had suffered in foreign lands.

In his book, *Faith in the future*, the British Chief Rabbi, Sir Jonathan Sacks, says 'The Hebrew Bible contains the great command, 'you shall love your neighbour as yourself' (Leviticus 19:18), and this has often been taken as the basis of biblical morality. But it is not: it is only part of it. The Jewish sages noted that on only one occasion does the Hebrew Bible command us to love our neighbour, but in 37 places it commands us to love the stranger. Our neighbour is one we love because he is like ourselves. The stranger is one we are taught to love precisely because he is not like ourselves'.

That is a remarkable piece of illumination, he says. 'Love your neighbour as yourself' is the instruction that is readily quoted. Hardly ever do we hear God's oft-repeated command to 'love the stranger'.

At the beginning of the Bible, we are told that God creat-ed all of us in God's image and likeness. Each human being is made in God's image – is an icon of God, regardless of culture, colour, class, creed, country of origin or gender. How we treat other people who are different from us or who are strangers is not only a matter of politics, social order, legislation or economics; it is also at the heart of our religious faith and practice, for how we treat others, espe-cially those who are different, is how we treat those who are made in God's image and likeness.

However, over the centuries, many different attitudes and ideologies have developed to divide and separate us despite out common humanity and contrary to the fundamental truth that we are all children of the one Father, God. In India, the caste system which separates people from one another is an integral part of religious structures and prac-tices. The theories of many races and of the purity of races which fail to understand that there is only one human race were developed into their worst forms in Nazi Germany in the last century and the doctrine of apartheid institution-alised racism in South Africa until the 1990s. In the pursuit of national exclusivity, 'ethnic cleansing' resulted in the deaths of hundreds of thousands of people in the Former Yugoslavia in recent decades, and sent many thousands more into neighbouring countries as refugees and asylum seekers.

Religion has often been used to support these ideologies of racism and hatred. In South Africa, the story of Noah, who spoke words of curse to his son Canaan, was used by white people to justify institutionalised discrimination against the majority black population. Other Biblical stories have given ammunition to racists, including the story of Abraham driving out his black wife, Hagar, and the story of Moses being criticised by Aaron and Miriam because he had married a black Cushite woman.

The Exodus and strangers

Over time, in the Bible, we see how the 'insiders' have land and privilege, while the 'outsiders' become the people without space and without privilege. They are referred to as the 'strangers,' the ones to whom the insiders owe nothing, the ones from whom the insiders should keep separate. The strangers are nameless and unwelcome. The biblical term for the 'strangers' in the Hebrew Bible is *Habiru*, an alternative rendering of Hebrew. The term Hebrew has roots in the word *abar* which means 'to cross over'. A Hebrew, therefore, is someone who crosses over boundaries in the quest for life. The Hebrews are the people who finally became the 'people of God' in the Old Testament. They are strangers, outsiders, and a threat in Egypt, the land of their exile and slavery.

The Exodus from Egypt is a defining moment for the Children of Israel. As strangers in a strange land they had been exploited as workers, forced into slavery, and threatened with extermination. But God heard their cry even when they did not know how to call him by name. Through God's intervention, they were called out of Egypt and into freedom.

But instead of rejoicing at the defeat of their former enemies, the people of Israel are reminded constantly that they 'were once aliens and slaves yourselves,' to 'love the stranger, for you were strangers in the land of Egypt,' and to 'love the alien as yourself, for you were aliens in the Land of Egypt' (Deuteronomy 10:19-22; Deuteronomy 24:17-22; Exodus 22:21-24; Exodus 23:6-9; Leviticus 19:33-34). Because of that defining experience, they are told 'to be merciful to the stranger in your midst. In particular, the resident alien is given particular religious and political rights and duties. The alien is entitled to a day of rest (Exodus 23:12); aliens are to be treated in the same way as citizens, to receive fair treatment and justice, and may even celebrate the Passover, which recalls God's intervention in the plight of strangers in a strange land (Leviticus 19:34); and the alien with no means of support is to be left with the gleanings in the field (Leviticus 23:22; Deuteronomy 24:19; Ruth 2). 'The Lord your God is God of gods and Lord of lords, the great God, mighty and awesome, who is not partial and takes no bribe, who executes justice for the orphan and the widow, and who loves the strangers, providing them with food and clothing. You shall also love the stranger, for you were strangers in the land of Egypt' (Deuteronomy 10:17-19).

Why should you love the stranger? Because God loves the stranger – and, remember, you were strangers in the land of Egypt. The Hebrew – the stranger in Egypt, to whom God showed love, is now required to love the stranger.

The stranger and the prophets

The prophetic writings in the Old Testament are marked by an awareness of others, which includes other nations as a living part of God's plan of salvation. Yahweh is not just the God of Israelites, but the God of all creation, and the salvation God offers to the Israelites is also offered to the Gentiles.

Isaiah illustrates how God's concern is for 'all the nations': 'He shall judge between the nations, and shall arbitrate for many peoples; they shall beat their swords into ploughshares, and their spears into pruning hooks; nations shall not lift up sword against nation, neither shall they learn war any more' (Isaiah 2:4).

Later, we are told God 'will make for all peoples a feast of rich food, a feast of well-aged wines, of rich food filled with marrow, of well-aged wines strained clear' (Isaiah 25:6), and that God's salvation will 'reach to the end of the earth' (Isaiah 49:6). There are no strangers in God's plan of salvation, as it unfolds for the Prophets, and Isaiah and other prophets call for a mission among the aliens (Isaiah 42:5 ff; Isaiah 66:19; Zechariah 14; Tobit 14:6). God cannot be confined to one ethnic group, and other nations, the strangers and aliens, are part of God's plan for the salvation of the whole of creation.

The experience of exile

With the capture of Jerusalem and the forced exile in Babylon, the Children of Israel once again become strangers and aliens in another land. Once again, they are reminded of the experience of their ancestors when they were aliens and strangers in Egypt. 'By the rivers of Babylon – there we sat down and there we wept when we remembered Zion'. Psalm 137 is the lament of the exiles, and is often studied in relation to refugees. The exiles went to Babylon as prisoners of war, the result of being on the losing side of a battle. Their longing for their home and their identity was refugee-like. But in their exile, the Israelites entered a formative and creative period. Their exile and oppression became a time of writing and reflection, in which they created their religious system, wrote down and edited their traditions and legal codes, drew up their religious laws, restated their identity, and established the synagogue.

The stranger in the New Testament

The first experience of the Holy Family is of being people being on the move, of a family that is homeless, and of a family that is forced into exile and to seek refuge. While Mary is still pregnant, she and Joseph are forced to leave their home because of a political decision, the taking of a census. But in Bethlehem they find there is no room for them, and Mary's child is born in a stable (Luke 2:1-7). After the visit of the wise men, Joseph had a vision and decided to flee to Egypt. The massacre of the innocents followed. After Herod's death, Mary and Joseph with the child Jesus returned to Nazareth (Matthew 2:13-15). In this story, the fear turns out to be well-founded, although in today's climate we might wonder whether Joseph could forward a credible story for an immigration officer. Matthew 2:9-22 illustrates a typical refugee's desire to go home when the threat recedes.

The traditions and legal codes the exiles brought back with them from Babylon made it impractical and impossible for religious and pious Jews in New Testament times to socialise and eat with outsiders and strangers, whose vessels and food were regarded as ritually unclean. But throughout his ministry, Jesus cuts through boundaries and separation between who is considered to be holy and profane. He eats with a tax collector (Mark 2:15-17), he allows a prostitute to wash his feet with her tears (Luke 7:36-50), and he heals the servant of a centurion or foreign official (Matthew 8:5-13; Luke 7:1-10; John 4:46-53) and the daughter of a Syro-Phoenician woman (Matthew 15:21-28, Mark 7:24-30).

The healing of the Syro-Phoenician woman's daughter marks a fundamental reorientation of the ministry and mission of Jesus, opening up the community of faith to the outsider and the stranger. Jesus' most subversive and radical activity, for which he is most criticised, is to eat with the outsiders, the social outcasts of his day. It is said that 'he eats with sinners and tax collectors'. The tax collectors were ostracised because they collaborated with the 'outsiders'.

Jesus expressed his solidarity with the poor and marginalized people of his day by eating with them. He welcomes the poor, 'the unclean,' 'the sinners,' the harlots and publicans and eats with them. In this he shows God's way, God's truth and God's life. He demonstrates a holiness of connectedness, not separateness, of intimacy, not aloofness. Jesus breaks down barriers, crosses our boundaries, includes those who would have been excluded, eats with anyone who would eat with him. Everything Jesus did and said demonstrated these things. He gives us examples of how to practise hospitality, how to eat with each other, and to eat with the most vulnerable ones. We are called to eat with 'the stranger'.

Jesus says that in welcoming the stranger, we welcome Christ himself: 'I was a stranger and you welcomed me … truly, I tell you, just as you did it to one of the least of these … you did it to me' (Matthew 25:42-45). And when Jesus dies on the Cross, when the disciples have fled, it falls to a stranger, the foreign centurion, to acknowledge openly who Jesus really is (Mark 15:39).

Welcoming the stranger is at heart of the Gospel message, at the heart of the story of the crucifixion and the resurrection. Indeed, when the Disciples on the road to Emmaus meet a stranger and invite him to eat with them, they find they are dining with Christ himself (Luke 24:13-35).

Strangers and the New Testament Church

Pentecost marks the birth of the Church. And at that birth, we read in the Acts of the Apostles, the first Christian proclamation was heard by a list of people from nations that represented the whole inhabited earth (Acts 2:1-13). As the early Church debated whether membership should be confined to those who were Jews by birth or by conversion or opened to embrace the stranger and the Gentile (Acts 10:1-43), the Apostle Peter proclaims the liberating words: 'I truly understand that God shows no partiality, but in every nation anyone who fears him and does what is right is acceptable to him' (Acts 10:34).

The early Church comes to see that everyone, without distinction, is a candidate for the kingdom, including those who have been ethnic outsiders and strangers. The Apostle Paul tells the church in Ephesus that there is no distinction between Jews and Gentiles because in Christ we have a new humanity which is one. 'So then you are no longer strangers and aliens, but you are citizens with the saints and also members of the household of God' (Ephesians 2:13). He writes to the Colossians that 'there is no longer Greek and Jew, circumcised and uncircumcised, barbarian, Scythian, slave and free; but Christ is all and in all'! (Colossians 3:11).

Towards the end of his mission, the Apostle Paul placed a very high value on hospitality to the stranger: 'Contribute to the needs of the saints; extend hospitality to strangers' (Romans 12:13). Similar values are expressed in other New Testament epistles: 'Beloved, you do faithfully whatever you do for the friends, even though they are strangers to you' (3 John 1:5). 'Do not neglect to show hospitality to strangers, for by doing that some have entertained angels without knowing it'.

3
Bible Studies

BIBLE STUDY 1

The hospitality of Abraham (Genesis 18:1-15)

ABRAHAM IS THE GREAT PATRIARCH OF THE OLD TESTAMENT, and his story is a key story in the Hebrew Bible. Abraham began life as a stranger and a wandering Aramean (Genesis 12; Deuteronomy 26:5), and his journey from Haran in modern Turkey to Bethel in Canaan was an epic journey (see Genesis 12:1-9). In his old age, Abraham finds himself one day sitting at the door of his tent, in the heat of the day. And unexpectedly he finds himself welcoming three strangers by the oaks of Mamre. He takes good care of them, he sits them down, he washes their feet, he brings them food and drink, and Sarah and Abraham find that in welcoming these strangers they are entertaining angels and receiving God as their guest. Sometimes the guests are referred to in the plural, but sometimes the story uses the singular form when we are told the Lord is appearing to Abraham, as Abraham addresses 'My Lord' and as we are told the Lord spoke.

As a consequence, God makes a promise to Sarah that at first seems laughable and unbelievable. But this is a key story in the unfolding of God's plans for all of humanity and all of creation.

This story is traditionally depicted in Orthodox iconography as a visit not by strangers or angels, but a visit by the Triune God. Hospitality is no mere human transaction – 'I was a stranger, and you welcomed me'. This story has resonances of the many meals Jesus will have with strangers in the New Testament, and an anticipation of the heavenly meal in the world to come. The promise to Sarah also anticipates the promise to Mary, one an old woman beyond the age of expecting a child, the other a young woman too young to expect a child. The story is reflected in the Letter to Hebrews: 'Let mutual love continue. Do not neglect to show hospitality to strangers, for in doing that some have entertained angels without knowing it' (Hebrews 13:1-2).

Points for discussion

This story brings together several strands of thinking about the stranger than recur again and again throughout the Bible. The promise to the patriarchs is a promise with universal significance; the command to love is a command not just to love God and to love our neighbour, but to love the stranger and the alien too; there are no ethnic boundaries in the kingdom. How welcome is the stranger in my church on a Sunday morning, or in my home? How would I feel when, just as I was looking for a moment's peace and quiet, I was disturbed by the arrival of three strangers? How far does my hospitality extend? How seriously do I listen to what strangers have to say to me?

BIBLE STUDY 2
Joseph and the immigrants (Genesis 41)

THIS STORY IS FULL OF STRANGERS. Joseph, who has been sold into slavery in Egypt by his brothers, begins his life as a slave, as a stranger, as a foreigner and an immigrant. It was not his choice to end up in Egypt, but then how many immigrants or refugees came to Ireland not by choice design but due to circumstances beyond their control? In the story of Joseph in Egypt, we read: 'They served him by himself, and them by themselves, because the Egyptians might not eat bread with the Hebrews, for that is an abomination to the Egyptians'. Nevertheless, Joseph rises to a position of privilege and power, and the man who was once an outsider becomes an insider, the man who was once a stranger now becomes known to all in power.

By means of his gifts, Egypt prepares well during seven years of plenty for seven years of famine that follow, and the man who was once a poor stranger and who arrived without anything he could call his own and who became a prisoner now becomes a blessing to the country in which he had found himself. Later on, long after the events in this passage, we read that a king arose in Egypt who 'did not know Joseph' (Exodus 1:8). This Pharaoh claimed the foreigners were becoming too many and planned to exterminate them (Exodus 1-2). He made life miserable for them, withholding the necessary materials while forcing them to make bricks. God hears their cry and heeds their suffering, and desires their freedom. But even then, they spend another forty years as wanderers and strangers in the wilderness.

Points for discussion

Read the story of Joseph in Genesis. Ask whether you know anyone who has arrived in this country penniless and without a choice of where they were going. Can you imagine someone who came to this country as a stranger but became a blessing? Can you think of people who left Ireland due to circumstances beyond their control but who became a blessing to their new home country? To help stimulate this discussion, you might think of Saint Patrick who came to Ireland first as a slave but later returned as a missionary, Eamon de Valera who was born in New York but became President of Ireland; or the many Irish emigrants in America whose family rose to fame, such as the Kennedys; or immigrants who later went home again and became a blessing to their own country, such as Kader Asmal who became a South African cabinet minister.

Joseph was forced to eat on his own because the Egyptians believed that to eat with the stranger would be defiling. Have the new strangers in our midst found themselves welcome in the homes you know? Discuss also how you enjoy the new ethnic restaurants and take-away outlets in your area. When you go there, do you ever ask the people who work there where they come from? Are they welcome in your church? Are their children welcome in your school?

Can you imagine the modern equivalent of foreigners being forced to make bricks without straw? You might like to consider the wages offered to East European building workers on some sites, or talk to some of the Chinese students working late hours in a local supermarket or filling station.

Try to write an imaginary conversation between a would-be refugee or illegal immigrant trying to justify a right of entry to immigration officers at the airport or a port.

BIBLE STUDY 3

Ruth

THE BOOK OF RUTH IS A COMPACT STORY of an uprooted family. Elimelech, from Bethlehem, and his wife Naomi emigrate to Moab, bringing their two sons with them. Eventually Naomi finds herself a widow in a strange land, and when both her sons die she is left dependent on two foreign daughters-in-law. One daughter-in-law, Orpah, returns to her own family, but the other daughter-in-law, Ruth, clings to her mother-in-law, telling Naomi: 'Where you go, I will go; where you lodge, I will lodge; your people will be my people, and your God my God' (Ruth 1:16).

Naomi and Ruth were destitute when they arrived in Bethlehem. Naomi is known to few people there, and the two widows find themselves poor strangers and exiles in a strange land. The system of gleaning, which allows the poor to garner some food from the corners of the fields at harvest time, allows Ruth to gather food for both of them. And while she is gleaning, she meets Boaz and they marry.

Two women who were exiles and strangers come to a new-found prosperity. Ruth gives birth to a son Obed, who is the grandfather of David, and the ancestor of Jesus. The stranger finds sympathy and love, and the love shown to the stranger becomes a blessing not just for Israel but for the whole world.

Points for discussion

What issues does the story raise? Try to imagine the story in today's setting, with a family leaving Ireland and returning with a 'foreign wife' or a family coming here and, beset by tragedy, returning home. How do we respond to those strangers in our midst who come to our doors asking for the gleanings of the field? How do you feel about the Roma women selling or begging with her children? What would have happened to God's plan of salvation if Ruth had decided not to go back to Bethlehem with Naomi, if Boaz had said no to Ruth's request, if Ruth had never married again?

BIBLE STUDY 4

The healing of a woman's daughter
(Matthew 15:21-28, or Mark 7:24-30)

A FTER A VERY TRYING AND BUSY TIME, Jesus tries to find some rest and quiet in the area of Tyre and Sidon – in territory associated with Elijah, the prophet who, in Kieran O'Mahony's words, 'was markedly, even offensively, open to foreigners'. his plans to retreat into hiding are frustrated when a woman from the region comes to him with very pressing demands. In Saint Matthew's account she is a Canaanite woman; in Saint Mark's telling of the story she is a Greek or Syro-Phoenician woman. In either case, she is a Gentile, a stranger, a foreigner, a Greek-speaker and a woman. Her religion, language, nationality and gender put her beyond the compassion of the disciples.

But Jesus refuses every effort to send her away. She is direct and aggressive in demanding healing and justice. And in demanding justice and healing for her daughter, she is demanding them for herself too. The dialogue between this woman and Jesus must have sounded crude and aggressive. She is a pushy woman, who forces herself into the house and with a touch of melodrama throws herself at the feet of Jesus, demanding he should heal her daughter. But Jesus appears to speak with contempt: he compares his fellow

Jews to 'little children,' while Gentiles are compared to dogs. Dogs were then regarded as unclean animals, and at the time it was a popular teaching that dogs were the only animals to be excluded with certainty from heaven.

The woman responds, perhaps with wry humour, with an image of children playing with puppy dogs, away from adult view, under the table. Jesus appreciates this encounter: her insistence on meeting Jesus face-to-face, her refusal to be oppressed because of ethnicity, religion, language or gender, as well as her forthright way of speaking and her subliminal but humorous comparisons are all part of the drama in this story.

And this combination produces results. In Saint Mark's Gospel, Jesus responds to her demands and, as a consequence, when she returns home she finds her child has been healed. In Saint Matthew's Gospel, Jesus goes further – he commends her for her faith and her daughter is healed instantly.

Points for discussion

The confrontation between this woman and Jesus, the way they enter dialogue with each other, and the consequences of that dialogue are important when we consider how we deal with strangers and foreigners. Do we find them pushy and demanding? How do we respond when the foreign woman in our society wants the same treatment in hospital as Irish-born children? How do we respond when foreigners who are more open and joyful in conversation, appear to be encroaching on our privacy on the bus, on the street or in a shop? Are we like the Disciple, and want to send them away? Or are we like Jesus, and engage in conversation with them? Do we think we have some privileges that should not be shared with the outsider and the stranger?

BIBLE STUDY 5

The Samaritan woman at the well (John 4)

THE SAMARITANS ARE RELIGIOUS AND CULTURAL OUTSIDERS for the Jewish people in the New Testament period. Although these two people share the same land, the Samaritans are strangers and outsiders. Although they share faith in the same God and share the same Torah (the first five books of the Bible), the Samaritans are seen as having a different religion. Jesus tries to break down those barriers. The Good Samaritan is not a stranger but is the very best example of a good neighbour (Luke 10:29-37). Among the ten lepers who are healed, only the Samaritan returns to give thanks, and this 'foreigner' is praised for his faith (Luke 17:11-19).

In this story in Saint John's Gospel, the Disciples are already doing something unusual: they have gone into the city to buy food; but this is no ordinary city – this is a Samaritan city, and any food they might buy from Samaritans is going to be unclean according to Jewish ritual standards. While the Disciples are in Sychar, Jesus sits down by Jacob's Well, and begins talking with a Samaritan woman who comes to the well for water. And their conversation becomes a model for how we respond to the stranger in our midst, whether they are foreigners or people of a different religion or culture.

Jesus presents the classical Jewish perception of what Samaritans believe and how they worship. The Samaritans accepted only the first five books of the Bible – the Pentateuch or Torah – as revealed scripture. For their part, Jews of the day pilloried this Samaritan refusal to accept more than the first five books of the Bible by claiming the Samaritans worshipped not the one God revealed in the five books but five gods. Jesus alludes to this – with a sense of humour – when he says the woman had five husbands.

In other circumstances, a Jewish man would have refused to talk to a Samaritan woman or to accept a drink form her hands; any self-respecting Samaritan woman would have felt she had been slighted by these comments and walked away immediately. Instead, the two continue in their dialogue: they talk openly and humorously with one another, and listen to one another. Jesus gets to know the woman and she gets to know Jesus. All dialogue involves both speaking and listening – speaking with the expectation that we will be heard, and listening honestly to what the other person is saying rather than listening to what our prejudices tell us they ought to say.

When the Disciples arrive back, they are filled with a number of questions but are so shocked by what is happening before them that they remain silent. Their silence reflects their inability to reach out to the stranger. But there are other hints at their failure and their prejudices: the woman gives and receives water as she and Jesus talk, but they fail to return with bread for Jesus to eat and they fail to feed into the conversation about faith and about life. They are still questioning and unable to articulate their faith, but the woman at least recognises Jesus as a Prophet. They made no contact with the people in Sychar, but she rushes back to tell the people there about Jesus. No one in the city was brought to Jesus by the disciples, but many Samaritans listened to what the woman had to say.

Points for discussion

The conversation between Jesus and the Samaritan woman is a model for all our encounters with people we see as different or as strangers. Am I like the Disciples, and too hesitant to go over and engage in conversation with the stranger who is at the same well, in the same shop, at the same bus stop? If am going to enter into conversation with the stranger, am I open to listening to them, to talking openly and honestly with them about where they come from and what they believe? When the conversation is over, will they remain strangers? How open am I to new friendships?

4
Worship material and resources

IF THE CHURCH IS TO SPEAK OUT against racism and disintegration, then we need to pray about those issues too. The diversity of church groups emerging among our new neighbours offers exciting new opportunities for worship and times together, especially on occasions such as the Week of Prayer for Christian Unity, Harvest, Racial Justice Sunday in September, or special days to mark peace or our witness against racism.

The Bible study units in Chapter 4 provide some ideas for readings and sermon topics. Other readings might include, from the Old Testament the following:

- Exodus 22:17 - 21 (Resident aliens in the Covenant Code)
- Leviticus 19:33- 34 (Resident aliens as part of the Holiness Code)
- Deuteronomy 24:17 - 22 (Resident aliens as part of the Justice Code)

And from the New Testament the following:

- Matthew 25:35-40 (Consideration for the 'least' among us)
- Luke 10:25-37 (the Good Samaritan)
- Luke 24:13-35 (the Stranger on the Road to Emmaus)

Words of Welcome

God bless our eyes so that we will recognise injustices.

God bless our ears so that we will hear the cry of the stranger.

God bless our mouths so that we will speak words of welcome to newcomers.

God bless our shoulders so that we will be able to bear the weight of struggling for justice.

God bless our hands so that we can work together with all people to establish peace.

From Cafod, the Catholic Agency for Overseas Development ©️ National Council of Churches of Australia, Protecting the Persecuted Liturgy, 2002

Collects

The collects provide a rich tradition in the Anglican Communion. Many of our collects are associated with specific Sunday rather than special themes, but can be used and adapted for special occasions.

Among the second collects in the *Book of Common Prayer 2004* worth considering include (page numbers are from the *Book of Common Prayer 2004*) are the following: the first Sunday of Christmas (p. 247); Epiphany (p. 249); fourth Sunday after Epiphany (p. 252); Second Sunday before Lent (p. 256); Sixth Sunday in Lent (p. 265); Maundy

Thursday (p. 269); Pentecost (p. 279); Thirteenth Sunday after Trinity (p. 291); Twentieth Sunday after Trinity (p. 296); Fourth Sunday before Advent (p. 299); and Third Sunday before Advent (p. 300). Other collects that can be adapted include those for mission (p. 334) and for unity (p. 335).

Intercessions

For the people and land from which refugees have fled, may there be peace and reconciliation between people and nations.

That strangers, refugees, and those who seek asylum may find a welcome among us.

We pray for all who make our laws and administer justice: may the God of justice be their guide.

We pray for those who minister to the vulnerable and broken people, especially the homeless and displaced: that they may show God's welcoming love.

We often feel powerless in the face of crushing poverty, injustice and violence in our world; we ask for the courage to reach out to victims of injustice and poverty.

Lord, you bestow on us the gift of your spirit in our lives to sustain our wavering hope.

Accept the prayers we make from the fullness of our hearts, and grant the requests we make with confidence in you. Through Christ our Lord.

From Cafod, the Catholic Agency for Overseas Development ©
Brentwood Diocese Refugee Week

Hymns

The Discovery Gospel Choir CD, *Made to be as one*, offers suitable material for liturgies on the theme of welcoming the stranger. But there are many suitable hymns in the *Irish Church Hymnal* for this theme, including the following:

3: God is love.

22: You shall cross the barren desert

31: Lord of the boundless curves and space.

466: Here from all nations, all tongues and all peoples.

494: Beauty for brokenness

496: For the healing of the nations

499: When I needed a neighbour, were you there, were you there?

500: Would you walk by on the other side?

501: Christ is the world's true light

502: God! As with silent hearts we bring to mind:

503: Make me a channel of your peace:

504: O let us spread the pollen of peace:

509: Your kingdom come, O God:

514: We cannot measure how you heal:

515: A new commandment I give unto you:

517: Brother, Sister, let me serve you:

522: In Christ there is no east or west:

532: Who are we who stand and sing?

5
What can we do?

OFTEN WE FIND IT DIFFICULT to move from knowledge to action. When we are faced with great global problems, such as world poverty and global warming, we know there are pressure groups and alliances, often supported by the churches and mission agencies, which bring these issues to the attention of politicians. But it is very difficult at times to deal with major problems at a local level. However, if we see the changing face of Ireland not as a problem to be solved but as a welcome opportunity to put our faith and discipleship into action, then there are many things we can do at a local, parish or diocesan level.

What do we do next?

The Immigration Council of Ireland reminds us that we need to accept that immigration in Ireland is a permanent reality and one that enhances our country and our nation. Facing this reality positively means respecting and supporting cultural and ethnic diversity in Ireland. Immigrants and immigrant communities in Ireland should be empowered to improve their quality of life. Ireland must comply with international laws, obligations, and undertakings in relation to immigration, legislation must be both humane and just, and the information provided to immigrants has to be readily accessible, accurate, clear, objective, and practical.

Getting to know your neighbour

The theme of this short book or resource pack has been 'welcoming the stranger' so that we might get to know the new angels in our midst in Ireland. Not all our new neighbours will want to be integrated into Irish society – many are hoping to return home when economic, political or political circumstances change at home. But whether they want to be integrated or not, all are in need of and deserve a welcome and acceptance.

If we are going to welcome these new arrivals, then we need to get to know them. We can find them in the new churches that have grown up in our towns and cities. Some of them have opened a variety of ethnic restaurants, but sadly we often fail to realise that eating is about more than feeding – eating is also about fellowship and welcome. Have you noticed the variety of new restaurants in your town or parish? Do you know anything about the families who own and run them, or about the workers employed there?

Some points for action

1. Prayer and worship

In the Dublin and Glendalough Dioceses, the Discovery Committee – the Diocesan Committee for the International Community – has been organising regular 'Discovery' services. These have been billed as 'Anglican worship with an African flavour,' and include African songs from the 'Discovery Gospel Choir,' African-style processions for the opening, offertory and closing, some African-style dancing and prayers in a number of African languages. Usually they are followed by informal, buffet-style meals with a variety of ethnic foods and fare on offer.

The 'Discovery' services usually take place in Saint George's and Saint Thomas's Church in Cathal Brugha Street, off O'Connell Street in the City Centre. Preachers with an African background at these services have included Archbishop Desmond Tutu from South Africa, Bishop Mouneer Hanna Anis of Cairo from Egypt, Bishop Jered Kalimba of Shyogwe from Rwanda, the Revd Obinna Ulogwara from Nigeria, now serving in Whitechurch and Tallaght parishes in Dublin, the Revd Kevin Ronne from South Africa who is Rector of Clane, Co Kildare, and the Revd Sahr Yambasu, a Methodist minister from Sierra Leone now serving in Galway. But other 'Discovery' services have taken place outside Dublin, sometimes with an 'Indian' flavour. They have included Indian music and prayers, with visiting preachers.

How inclusive is the worship you take part in? Are we aware in our prayers of the needs of others? And are we aware of the needs of others to pray in other styles as well as other languages? In our after-worship gatherings, can we go beyond the traditional offering of tea or coffee and chocolate biscuits? If you invited some of our new residents to bring along some food for an after-church buffet, how far would this go in helping us to know and love our neighbours? A parish buffet dinner, with food from many countries and continents, offers a fun time for all and a real opportunity to nurture new friendships and to broaden horizons.

2. Worshipping with your neighbour

Some parishes already know that sharing church buildings with other denominations has been an enriching experience. Instead of seeing their churches being used by strangers, they have found themselves with a ready-made opportunity to get to their new neighbours. Some of the most recent examples in Dublin include the former Church of Ireland parish church in Harold's Cross, which has become a parish church for the Russian Orthodox Church;

Christ Church, Leeson Park, which is being used by the Romanian Orthodox Church; and Saint Maelruain's, Tallaght, and St Ann's Dawson Street, which occasionally host congregations from the Indian Orthodox Church. Learning from your neighbours about the riches of their liturgy and spirituality teaches us a very humbling lesson: we soon realise that welcoming the stranger is not just about meeting their demands but about discovering that we have many needs that must be met too. It's not always them demanding from us. We have much to gain from their spirituality and their openness in worship.

But we can also learn from those who are not Christians. For example, from Muslims we can learn the need for simplicity in expressing the core beliefs at the heart of our faith; we can come to appreciate the comfort of a daily rhythm of prayer in our lives and the need for humility in body and soul when we approach God in prayer; we can learn about the true meaning of charity; they can remind us of the value of returning once again to the practice and exercise of fasting; and they can help us to recover the symbolism and spirituality of pilgrimage.

Even when we find it is wise not to or it is difficult to consider sharing with our neighbours at their time of worship, we often learn from the simplicity or the majesty of the places of worship they build for themselves, and we can enjoy the social times built around their special days or festivals. The mosques in Dublin have shops and restaurants that offer an array of fare and an opportunity to taste the foods of people from a vast variety of countries.

3. Parish and diocesan organisations

Is there a welcoming, smiling face in your church porch every Sunday morning? Do our new immigrants know they are welcome in our churches and at parish gatherings? Is your parish vestry representative of the new, changing profile of the Church? Have you elected new parish members to your diocesan synod? If their voice is not heard at diocesan level, how can your diocesan councils take heed of their needs when it comes to discussing education, mission, social action and outreach? Are we providing the necessary support and resources for our parish schools and our diocesan secondary schools to combat racism and to promote inclusiveness?

4. Hospitals and schools

In many hospitals and nursing homes throughout Ireland, the medical, nursing and ancillary staffs have a higher proportion of foreign-born workers than can be found among the patients. But in many hospitals there is an expectation that the Church of Ireland chaplain will look after all the patients of 'other faiths'. Who looks out for the needs of hospital staff who come from different backgrounds? Who sees that their religious and dietary needs are catered for in hospital canteens and restaurants? Who asks whether they have appropriate places to pray or whether they are allowed time off for appropriate cultural or religious festivals?

The same needs must be identified among the pupils – and the parents – in our parish and diocesan run schools. School meals may need to have more variety and those involved in providing them may need to ask whether they need to show more sensitivity. Teachers may have to take account of the difficulty faced by older students who are fasting during daylight hours in the month of Ramadan. When Ramadan falls in winter, this may be difficult for children feeling the biting cold weather. During the summer, this may be even more complicated, especially when Ramadan falls at the same time as summer exams, such as the Leaving and Junior Certificate.

5. Speak up and sign up

But don't wait at the front door of our house, your church or your school to meet your new neighbours. Call on them and let them know they are welcome; ask them about their needs; and offer a friendly welcome and a voice that is willing to speak up on their behalf.

Your parish, church group, school or community can sign up for the National Action Plan Against Racism (NPAR). The NPAR originates from commitments given by the Irish Government and other governments at the United Nations World Conference Against Racism in South Africa in 2001. The decision to develop the NPAR was further reaffirmed in Sustaining Progress, the Social Partnership Agreement 2003-05. The emphasis throughout the Plan is on developing reasonable and common sense measures to accommodate cultural diversity in Ireland.

But we can also sign up when local petitions are being organised against racism or protesting against deportations that appear to be unfair or not to take account of family or special circumstances. We can speak up when people in our area are being paid low wages or forced to work longer hours because others realise their foreignness makes them vulnerable and often leaves them without anyone to listen to their complaints or to speak up on their behalf.

6. Language assistance

Does the language of our worship and of the hymns we use in our churches reflect the diversity of people who worship in your parish or who should feel welcome in your church? The recent survey by academics at the National University of Ireland Maynooth, which showed that over

167 languages are being used in everyday conversations in Ireland, also identified the lack of translation services as a serious issue for thousands of people living in Ireland. According to Mary Phelan of Dublin City University there is a huge demand for interpreters by state authorities, but little focus on the standards of translation. The need for quality English-language tuition for students at all education levels is also an urgent need, according to Mary Ruane of University College Dublin.

Has your parish identified the language needs of people in your congregation? Have you explored the resources in liturgy and hymns available in some of the languages that are spoken widely throughout Ireland today?

Are there people in your parish who could help provide translation services for people who need them? Are there members of your congregation who could volunteer to provide good quality English language tuition for people trying to integrate into Irish society?

Conclusion

Ideas need words to convey their depth and meaning. Without getting to know our neighbours we cannot know their hopes and fears, their needs and aspirations. Welcoming and getting to know our neighbours is a two-way process. It involves them and it involves us. And it is mutually enriching. By welcoming the new strangers in Irish society we will find out more about ourselves, but we will also be enriching the spirituality, the culture and the resources of this island nation.

Some of the strangers we welcome will eventually go home and, depending on the welcome they receive from us, will become involved in the life of the churches in their own home areas. By getting to know the stranger we will be unwittingly enriching the life of the church in other countries ... we will be engaged in a truly missionary enterprise.

But some of those strangers will stay on in Ireland, and will contribute greatly to the social, cultural, political, economic and religious life of this island. Their children will marry our children, and their grandchildren will be our grandchildren. In welcoming strangers we will soon discover we are bringing angels into our churches and into our families.

6
Useful resources & publications

ORGANISATIONS:

Access Ireland Refugee Social Integration Project

Dominick Court, 40/41 Dominick Street Lower, Dublin 1
Telephone: 01-8780589 Fax: 01-8780591

Access Ireland aims to promote the integration of refugees in a way that highlights their positive contribution to Irish society. It promotes access to health and social services by promoting greater understanding of refugee needs and multi-cultural diversity amongst service providers and local communities. Access Ireland also seeks to support the development of community initiatives among refugee groups.

http://www.accessireland.ie/

Association of Refugees and Asylum Seekers in Ireland (ARASI)

19 Belvedere Place, Dublin 1. Telephone: 01-8552111

ARASI is an umbrella organisation for all community based refugee organisations dealing with refugees and asylum seekers issues. The organisation is run by volunteers who are asylum seekers, refugees, and Irish people.

Churches Asylum Network (CAN)

The Refugee Project, Columba Centre, Maynooth, Co Kildare. Telephone: 01-5053157

Discovery (Dublin and Glendalough Diocesan Committee for the International Committee)

Contact c/o Whitechurch Vicarage, Whitechurch Road, Rathfarnham, Dublin 16. Provides advice on organising multicultural worship. The Discovery Gospel Choir was voted the 'Best Soul Music' by *Dubliner* magazine in 2005 and produces a number of resources, including a CD, *Made to be as one*, with songs from America, Ireland, Nigeria, South Africa, Sudan and Uganda.

Diversity Ireland, the National Action Plan Against Racism (NPAR)

Emphasises developing reasonable and common sense measures to accommodate cultural diversity in Ireland. The website has resources for education, news about intercultural events, information about grants available for work to combat racism, and valuable links.

www.diversityireland.ie/Home/Home_Page/index.html

The Equality Authority

2 Clonmel Street, Dublin 2. Public Information Centre Local: 1890-245-545 Telephone: 01-4173333

The Equality Authority is an independent body set up under the Employment Equality Act 1998, which outlaws discrimination in employment, vocational training, advertising, collective agreements, the provision of goods and services and other opportunities to which the public generally have access on nine distinct grounds.

www.equality.ie

Immigrant Council of Ireland

2 St Andrew Street, Dublin 2
Information service: 01-6740200
Administration: 01-6740202

The Immigrant Council of Ireland is a national independent non-governmental agency responding to the needs of immigrants in Ireland. It was established by Social Innovations Ireland, an organisation set up by Sister Stanislaus Kennedy in 2001, which works to demonstrate and create new innovative responses to changing social needs in Ireland. The Joint Steering Committee of the Immigrant Council of Ireland is made up of individuals who have expertise, interest and commitment in the area of immigration. The Council provides information on immigration issues such as:work permits, work visas and work authorisations; business permits; student visas; tourist visas and visitors' visas; permission to remain in Ireland; family reunification; citizenship and residency; regularisation; and voluntary return.

www.immigrantcouncil.ie

Integrating Ireland: the National Network of Refugee, Asylum Seeker and Immigrant Support

Contact c/o Comhlámh, 10 Upper Camden Street, Dublin 2. Telephone: 01-4783490

Integrating Ireland is an independent network of community and voluntary groups working in mutual solidarity to promote and realise the human rights, equality and full integration in Irish society of asylum seekers, refugees and immigrants. Established in 2000, the membership-based network currently comprises of over 190 organisations from all over Ireland, North and South.

www.integratingireland.ie

Irish Chinese Information Centre

63 Fitzwilliam Square Dublin 2

Telephone: 01-6114666

Irish Refugee Council

88 Capel Street, Dublin 1 Telephone: 01-8730042

www.irishrefugeecouncil.ie

Islamic Cultural Centre of Ireland

19 Roebuck Road, Clonskeagh, Dublin 14
Telephone: 01-2080000
www.iccislam.org

Islamic Foundation of Ireland

163 South Circular Road, Dublin 8
Telephone: 01-4533242
www.islaminireland.com

National Consultative Committee on Racism and Inter-Culturalism

www.nccri.ie

Refugee Information Service (RIS)

27 Annamoe Terrace, off North Circular Rd, Dublin 7

www.ris.ie

Telephone: 01-8382740

The RIS exists to counter social exclusion through the provision of a specialist information, referral and advocacy service to asylum-seekers and refugees. It is a free, confidential and independent information, advocacy and referral service for the refugee and asylum seeking community. The service is provided on an outreach clinic basis in areas of Dublin and Galway where refugees and asylum-seekers live in significant numbers.

Currently the RIS operates seven clinics in Dublin; Rialto, Amiens Street, Green Street, Blanchardstown, Tallaght, Rathmines and Manor Street. The RIS operates two clinics in Galway city.

Spiritan Asylum Services Initiative (SPIRASI)

213 North Circular Road, Dublin 7

Telephone: 01-8389664

SPIRASI is a humanitarian intercultural NGO formed in 1999 to meet the needs of asylum seekers and refugees in Ireland. It provides a range of services including counselling and other medical services for victims of torture, English classes and IT training, health information for other asylum seekers and refugees, offers English Language Education; information and communications; public awareness education; centre for the care of survivors of torture; research and publications programme; and community links programmes.

http://www.spirasi.ie/

PUBLICATIONS:

Asyland: the magazine of the Irish Refugee Council

Ursula Fraser and Colin Harvey (eds.), *Sanctuary in Ireland* (Dublin: Institute of Public Administration, 2004)

Steve Garner, *Racism in the Irish experience* (London: Pluto Press, 2004)

Roger Hooker and Christopher Lamb, *Love the stranger: Christian ministry in multi-faith areas* (London: SPCK, 1986)

Patricia Kelleher and Carmel Kelleher, *Voices of immigrants: the challenges of inclusion* (Dublin: Immigrant Council of Ireland, 2004)

Fee Ching Leong, *The experiences, expectations and aspirations of black and minority ethnic people in relation to the churches' role in tackling racism* (The All-Ireland Churches' Consultative Meeting on Racism, November 2005)

Alan V. Martin, 'The Ephesian moment: the possibilities of cultural reconciliation in a cosmopolitan environment', in Bernard Treacy (ed.), *No longer strangers* (Dublin: Dominican Publications, 2006)

Andrew G. McGrady (ed), *Welcoming the stranger: practising hospitality in contemporary Ireland* (Dublin: Veritas, 2006)

Kieran O'Mahony, *What the Bible says about strangers* (Maynooth: Irish Commission for Justice and Peace; and Belfast: Irish Council of Churches, 1999; 2002)

Bernard Treacy (ed.), *No longer strangers: cultural integration in Church and society in Ireland* (Dublin: Dominican Publications, A Doctrine & Life Special, 2006)

Welcoming angels. Report of the Archbishop's working group on combating racism (Dublin: Church of Ireland Dioceses of Dublin and Glendalough, 2005)